Detail of Christchurch and its surrounds. From *Greenwood's Map of Hampshire, 1825-6.*

CHRISTCHURCH
A Pictorial History

Christchurch Quay, *c*.1900.

CHRISTCHURCH
A Pictorial History

Christine Taylor

Phillimore

1994

Published by
PHILLIMORE & CO. LTD.
Shopwyke Manor Barn, Chichester, Sussex

ISBN 0 85033 901 4

Printed and bound in Great Britain by
BIDDLES LTD.
Guildford, Surrey

List of Illustrations

Frontispiece: Christchurch Quay, *c.*1900

issued for the demolition of the castle. The after effects of both the Reformation and the Civil War eventually led to the demise of the town.

After this, Christchurch suffered neglect and dwindled to a small fishing town. A scheme to improve the town was investigated in the 17th century by the Earl of Clarendon, the Lord of the Manor. He proposed to make the River Avon navigable from Salisbury to Christchurch and had an Act drawn up in 1675-6 for the purpose. This scheme never came into fruition. The nearby harbour and the close proximity of the New Forest, however, enabled Christchurch to develop a new industry of smuggling, an activity that continued until the 19th century when the reduction in duty tax dramatically cut into the profits to be gained from contraband. Although a large number of families had some involvement with this rather dubious activity, smuggling was not the only occupation of the time. Fishing was still an important industry in the 19th century, as was work in the local breweries and on the land. Other industries included glove making, knitting stockings and the manufacture of fusee watch chains.

Twentieth-century Christchurch has retained much of its historic past. The High Street still follows the line of its Saxon foundations and the ancient origins of the town have been remembered in the name of the small shopping centre, Saxon Square. A number of the buildings around the priory are of medieval origin, others are later, but the historic integrity of the streets has remained intact.

Although the town has never played a major role in historic events, it has nevertheless retained a pride in its past. This pride was recently demonstrated in the 1994 celebrations marking the 900th anniversary of the priory.

Today Christchurch receives many visitors and despite being close to the sea is not a seaside town, but a pleasant town with great historical character.

Local Government and Public Services

The earliest recorded mayor of Christchurch was John Bevyll who held office in the 15th century. Prior to this date, a similar function was carried out by reeves who are thought to have been appointed by the Lord of the Manor. For the next 400 years, the Lord of the Manor had a say in the appointment of the new mayor and it was not until the town was made a borough in 1886, by Royal Charter, that the town council was able to elect its own mayor. The town had been made a municipal borough in 1882 under the Municipal Corporations Act.

The 19th century, particularly the latter part, saw great changes in the town. Public subscription led to areas of Christchurch being paved for the first time in the 1830s. Until this was completed the roads were little more than dirt tracks that needed to be watered, especially during dry weather, in order to keep dust from blowing around the streets.

A major contribution to street safety was the installation of gas lamps, which replaced the former oil lamps that lined the roads at night. The gas works, which came into use in 1853, were able to provide street lighting, initially in Bridge Street where the works were situated, and then for the whole town. Gas remained the principle form of street lighting until the 1930s, despite the opening of a branch, in 1903, of the Bournemouth and Poole Electricity Supply Company at Bargates.

Sanitation was a major problem in Christchurch as the rivers provided the town with both drinking water and a means of waste disposal. In the late 19th century, some houses had a water pump, but many people had to use the street pumps. A pump removed from Church Street in the 1860s caused an outcry and was reinstated in 1870. It was not until the end of the 19th century that the problem was properly addressed. A new waterworks which opened at Knapp piped water into homes for the first time and a sewage system was laid through the town providing the inhabitants of Christchurch with a solution to its sanitation problems.

A Parliamentary Act passed in 1774 required the town to provide a fire pump. In the early days, fire engines were kept in the church porch and at the insurance agents in Bridge Street. Long poles for the quick removal of burning thatch from buildings were hung in readiness under the Town Hall. Fires were a frequent hazard in the 19th century; two noteworthy fires occurred in the Bargates area in 1825 and 1864. On both occasions a number of families found themselves homeless. Gradually matters improved and, between March 1905 and March 1906, there were no fires in Christchurch that required the attendance of the fire brigade. The volunteers, however, were still paid for attending four practice drills and the accounts show that the total payments for the entire brigade came to £9 8s. during that year.

Road, Rail and Public Transport

Although the first stage coach ran through Christchurch in 1640, it was not until the 19th century that the demand for commercial and public transport increased. In 1857, a new omnibus route went into operation. This ran from the *King's Arms Hotel* in Bridge Street to Mudeford and was operated by Nicholas Newlyn, the proprietor. Fares were 6d. each way.

Towards the end of the 19th century, goods were transported from Christchurch by a carrier service. John Tilley of Castle Street ran carriers to Southampton on Thursday mornings, returning the next day. A daily service was operated to Southbourne, Bournemouth and Poole by E. and J. Burt, while John Jubbs's carrier went to Salisbury via Ringwood and Fordingbridge. The increased volume of traffic soon meant that the medieval Town Bridge, in Bridge Street, became congested with carriages and carriers and had to be widened in 1899.

In 1847, trains came to the area for the first time. The nearest station at this time was at Holmsley and passengers had to be taken by omnibus to their final destination. It was not until a few years later, in 1862, that the town of Christchurch opened its own station.

On 17 October 1905, the first trams ran through the streets of Christchurch. The power to run them was supplied by the newly formed Bournemouth and Poole Electricity Supply Company, which had premises in Bargates. The trams continued to run to Poole until 8 April 1936, when the first trolley bus ran through the streets of the town. Unlike the trams, where the driver changed seats and drove the vehicle from the other end in order to move in the opposite direction, the trolley buses had to have space to turn. The lack of space in Church Street led to an ingenious solution to the problem and a turntable was built behind the *Dolphin Inn*. The last trolley bus stopped running on 20 April 1969.

Local Industries

The two rivers running through Christchurch and its harbour and the nearby coastline have provided the town with several industries over the centuries. The Stour and Avon provided the power to drive the wheels of the mills positioned along their banks. The rivers and the sea also provided a plentiful source of fish, particularly salmon for which Christchurch was famous.

During the late 18th and 19th centuries, an important local industry was that of fusee watch chain making. These tiny chains were used to ensure that watches and clocks kept even time as they wound down. There were three chain manufacturers in Christchurch,

Robert Harvey Cox, Henry Jenkins and William Hart. The latter two manufacturers employed over two hundred local residents, many of whom were women who worked from home. Robert Harvey Cox, on the other hand, employed children from a number of workhouses in the area, including Christchurch workhouse. The fusee chains manufactured in the town were supplied to the London, Birmingham and Liverpool watch and clock makers.

Another 19th-century local industry was the mining of ironstone boulders or 'doggers' from the upper beds of Hengistbury Head. Ironstone, extracted by the Hengistbury Mining Company, was sent in barges towed by a steamer to Southampton, before being sent on to its destination in Wales. The removal of the more easily accessible boulders from the foreshore, however, led to quite severe erosion problems. James Druitt, mayor of Christchurch, expressed his concern that Bridge Street and other parts of the town would be flooded if mining activities continued. Eventually, ironstone extraction became unprofitable and mining came to a stop.

Many Christchurch industries were local affairs concerned, in the main, with providing services to the population of the town. It was not until the second half of the 20th century that larger industries, such as the Military Engineering and Experimental Establishment (MEXE), Signals Research Development Establishment (SRDE) and Airspeed, later taken over by De Havilland, came to the area.

Today MEXE has become the Military Vehicle Experimental Establishment (MVEE) and the sites occupied by the other industries have since been replaced by industrial and housing estates.

Health, Public Welfare and Education

The earliest hospital in Christchurch was the Leper Hospital or Lazar House, which was situated in Magdalen Lane, off Barrack Road. It was built to cope with leprosy during the early medieval period, when the disease was common to many towns. As the disease gradually died out, the hospital was used to look after the sick and injured in the town. It was eventually demolished *c*.1847. The hospital still in use today was originally built as the parish workhouse, after the first workhouse became too small to accommodate its occupants.

During the 18th century, several Acts of Parliament were drawn up to deal with the problem of housing the poor. A poor house was built in Christchurch in 1763 at Pitts Deep, now Quay Road. The building later became a workhouse and its inmates were put to work on a variety of tasks, including knitting hose, spinning and making the fusee watch chains for which Christchurch was famous during the 19th century. One member of the Workhouse Vestry Committee was Robert Harvey Cox, who had a chain-making business in the town and employed a number of children in the workhouse to make chains for him. Eventually the building became too small to house its ever growing number of inmates, so a new workhouse was built in 1880 at Fairmile to designs by C.C. Creeke and H. Burton. The estimated cost for building the new workhouse was approximately £12,000, though the eventual cost rose to £47,742.

A number of charities were set up in the town over the years, the oldest being the Magdalen Charity, which distributed quarterly payments to 25 'poor, sick, infirm, diseased and maimed' people of the old borough. Other charities, of which there were a number, were also aimed at helping the needy by providing clothing (Lyne's, Oakes, White's and Browne's), money (Brander's, Coffin's, Olive's and Williams') and food (Browne's and Elliott's). One charity, set up by John Clingan, helped to pay the apprenticeship fees for 10 children.

The earliest school in Christchurch was founded *c*.1140 and, as in many towns, disappeared with the dissolution of the monasteries. The need for some form of schooling and education led to the founding of the Free School, which was held in St Michael's Loft in the priory. This was established in 1662 as a free grammar school for local children and continued until 1828, when it became a private academy controlled by the vicar. It closed in 1869 when schooling became more widely available through the National Schools which were being set up throughout the country. In addition to the Free School, there were a number of private and boarding schools in the town which were attended by the children of families who could afford the fees.

The first National Schools in Christchurch were established in 1828 and opened the following year for 490 children. They were built in the High Street on land given to the mayor and burgesses by Sir George Henry Rose. A report of 1831 noted that a total of 354 pupils attended the schools. There was a clothing society in the girls school and the pupils contributed one penny per week. Clothes were sold to the children just before Whit Sunday and in October. The buildings were sold for £340 to James Druitt in 1866 who built a private residence on the site. The new schools were erected in Wick Lane.

Another school established almost at the same time as the National Schools was the Congregational or Independent school in Millhams Street. A day school was started in the early 19th century and enlarged in 1880 to accommodate 400 pupils. The attached infant school and school mistress's cottage were presented to the Dissenters by William Rowlett in 1834. The Independent school closed in 1926 when Clarendon Road infant school, situated between Barrack Road and Fairmile, opened with its intake of 325 children.

For more advanced training, a Science, Art and Technical school was inaugurated in 1898. This had its headquarters in the Town Hall and classes were held in various halls around the town. Courses included cookery, dress-cutting, ambulance, shorthand, carpentry and woodcarving

Military History

Towards the end of the 18th century, the Prime Minister, William Pitt, became concerned that an invasion by France was a very real threat. As a result barracks were built in a number of towns, especially those on the south coast. Christchurch barracks were built just outside the town, along a track (now Barrack Road) which led to Iford Bridge.

Christchurch had a number of volunteer units, including the Loyal Christchurch Volunteer Artillery, who are thought to have been based at the newly built barracks. One volunteer unit known to have been at the barracks in 1795 was the Christchurch Troop of the South Hampshire Volunteer Yeomanry Calvary. The 10th Hampshire Rifle Volunteers (later the 4th Volunteer Battalion of the Hampshire Regiment) were formed in 1860 when the threat of a surprise invasion by France became a real possibility.

The outbreak of the First World War gave rise to an enthusiastic response in the town. The workhouse was converted into the Christchurch Red Cross hospital and fund-raising events were held to raise money for the provision of equipment. A Union Jack Club was set up in the High Street, next to what is now Barclays' bank. The club served refreshments to the soldiers stationed at the barracks. Civilian volunteers were drafted to assist with stretcher bearing the wounded from the station to the hospital. Another event during the First World War was 'Thanksgiving Week' which was originally called 'Gun Week'. This was organised by the National War Savings Committee and raised money for war bonds.

Not long after the end of the First World War, the Experimental Bridging Establishment was set up at Christchurch barracks by the Royal Engineers. One notable achievement developed here which proved important to the Second World War effort was the Bailey bridge, invented by Sir Donald Bailey. Approximately two hundred miles of this type of bridge are thought to have been manufactured. The Experimental Bridging Establishment was later renamed the Military Engineering and Experimental Establishment (MEXE) in 1946.

Aircraft were also built just outside the town by Airspeed (later amalgamated with De Havilland). The site for this activity took place at Christchurch airfield, formerly a flying club. Part of this site was also given over to the Signals Research Development Establishment (SRDE), who conducted experiments with radar and radio beam detection. The SRDE was formed during the First World War and developed the first British guided weapons towards the end of the Second World War.

Around the Borough

The Borough of Christchurch stretches up to Hurn Forest in the north and to Walkford in the east. For several miles along the east and west sides of the borough the rivers Stour and Avon form a natural boundary and their estuary, which leads into Christchurch Harbour, makes up the southern boundary.

Some of the villages that make up the Borough of Christchurch have been illustrated in the following pages. Those not included have not been forgotten but merely demonstrate gaps in the collections of the Red House Museum and other photographic sources.

Fabric of the Past

.   Looking down on the town from the priory tower. The castle keep can be seen quite clearly. To the right of the keep
s the *King's Arms Hotel* and beyond that is the River Avon, wending its way into the distance. Many of the fields and
meadows in the background have since been built up.

2. A picturesque view of Christchurch which can still be seen today. Apart from the ivy covering the Constable's House (in the foreground), the castle and priory remain almost unchanged from when this photograph was taken at the turn of the 20th century. These two buildings, along with the castle keep, are in the former centre of the town and are the oldest remains still standing in Christchurch. The river in the foreground is the Avon and the water running in the background is the mill stream, which was used to power the town mill.

3. The Constable's House, one of the few Norman buildings remaining in Britain which has retained its chimney and garderobe (latrine). It was built to accommodate the residents of the castle as the keep (seen to the right) had become uncomfortable to live in.

4.   The old Town Hall on its former site at the junction of Castle Street and Church Street, *c*.1840. It was built in 1745-6 on the site of several houses and the shambles (butchers or slaughterhouses). After its removal to its present location in the High Street, a number of the arches were filled in. The cupola used to house a market bell but, as the market had dwindled in size, this was not replaced. Another feature that was not reinstated was the clock, which can just be seen on the cupola. The etching is by Benjamin Ferrey.

5.   The new position of the Town Hall in the High Street. It was moved to its present site in 1859. A need for office space led to one aspect of the removal scheme being neglected, that of the provision of a large room for meetings. In 1902, several additions were made to the building, including the parapet and balcony. Since this photograph was taken, most of the arches have been reinstated and the Civic Offices transferred to new premises in Bridge Street.

6. A view of the High Street in 1865, showing the principal means of obtaining water for domestic and commercial use—a water pump. The water was contaminated by sewage and was often unfit for drinking. Just behind the pump can be seen the remains of rubble created during the removal of the old Town Hall to its site in the High Street.

7. The opening of the new waterworks by the 4th Earl of Malmesbury in 1895. The waterworks was built near the site of Knapp Mill and provided piped water to the town for the first time. In 1920, the West Hampshire Water Company, who owned the site, bought Knapp Mill along with nine and a half acres of land from its owner, Miss Mary Francis Mills, for £2,000.

. Laying of the sewerage system in Beaconsfield Road at the beginning of the 20th century. The main system was laid hroughout the town in 1902, and greatly assisted in preventing the water supply from becoming contaminated.

9.   Ye Deluge, a horse-drawn, hand operated fire pump. This was owned and used by Christchurch barracks until it was bought by the Corporation for £15 in 1863. The lettering on the side of the pump states that it 'attended the Great Fire of London'. It is now housed at the Hampshire County Council Museums Service, prior to display at the Red House Museum and Gardens. The gentleman posing next to the fire pump is thought to be Thomas McArdle, a road contractor, who lived in Wick Lane in the 1930s.

10.   Members of Christchurch fire brigade. The men were all volunteers and the brigade relied entirely on donations from the public for the provision of uniforms and equipment. The town council was liable for repairs to the engine station and engine.

11. Sergeant Davis of the Hampshire Constabulary, who was stationed at Christchurch in the 1860s and lived in Millhams Street. The police station at this time was situated in Bargates.

12. A late 19th-century poster offering a reward in return for information leading to the recovery of mainly silver effects stolen from premises in the town.

£5 REWARD.

STOLEN

From CHRISTCHURCH, between the hours of 11 p.m. on Saturday and 8 a.m. on Sunday last, the following :

10 Silver Tablespoons, 6 Large and 6 Small Silver Forks, a large old-fashioned Silver Skewer, a Silver Crumb Scoop, a Silver Bread Fork, a Silver Butter Knife, a Plated-silver pair of very handsome Fish Servers in old Sheffield Plate, various Plated-Silver Dessert Knives and Forks, Fish Knives, etc., a Silver Patch Box (oval, about 2in. long, "A.W." on the back), a Silver Patch Box (round, about the size of half-a-crown), a Silver Vinaigrette (round, "F.F." on the top), a Silver Vinaigrette (oval, no initials), a Silver Vinaigrette (oblong, no initials, slightly arched), a Silver Vinaigrette (oblong, marked "I" or "II"), a Small Round Clock, a Gun-Metal Case of Compressed Medicines (very like a cigarette case in appearance).

THE ABOVE REWARD will be paid to any Person giving such inform-ation as will lead to the recovery of the articles and the conviction of the thief. Application to be made to the Christchurch Police Station.

MARSHALL, PRINTER, "TIMES" OFFICE, CHRISTCHURCH.

CHRISTCHURCH GAS COMPANY.

WORKS:

Rotten Row, Christchurch.

—

The Company will be pleased to fix the Cooking Stove (as illustration) **FREE OF CHARGE**. for the following hire:

No.	Per Quarter.
131	**1/-**
133	**1/6**
136	**2/6**
150	**4/-**

Complete with Enamel Crown Plate.

—

For further particulars apply to

Wm. DUNN,
MANAGER.

13. An advertisement for Christchurch Gas Company. The company opened in 1853 at Rotten Row and oversaw the installation in the town of gas lamps from Waterloo Bridge to the High Street. Prior to this, oil lamps were used for street lighting. The company later became a branch of the Bournemouth Gas and Water Company Limited.

14. An advertisement for Bournemouth and Poole Electricity Supply Company. The Bargates premises opened in 1903 and two years later was able to supply electricity for the running of the trams through Christchurch.

15. Workmen installing electric lighting in the priory in June 1934. Although electric lighting had been installed in some houses in Christchurch for a number of years, many premises and street lights had yet to convert to electricity.

16.   A four-in-hand coach at the junction of the High Street, Castle Street and Church Street, *c*.1899. Such coaches carried the mail and also provided transport for people living further out of the town. A former mayor of Christchurch, William Tucker, recalled in his reminiscences that he had seen as many as 'five or six four-in-hands in the High Street at one time'. The lettering on the left-hand side of the van behind the four-in-hand is an advertisement for W.E. Moorey, auctioneer and valuer.

17.   Junction of Castle Street and Church Street, *c.*1910. Horses and carriages are the only forms of transport and the roads are almost empty of traffic. The building on the left is the Wiltshire and Dorset bank which was built on the site of the *White Hart* public house. Today it is Lloyds bank.

18.   Repairs being made to the Town Bridge in 1937. The increase in the volume of traffic had caused this medieval bridge to subside. To enable work to be carried out on the crumbling foundations, a dam had to be built and the water pumped from under the arches. The pump and the flow of the diverted water can be seen clearly in the photograph.

19.   Christchurch railway station. Although a line had opened between Southampton and Dorchester in 1847, it by-passed Christchurch and Poole as the costs of taking it there were considered too expensive. A station called *Christchurch Road* at Holmsley was the nearest to Christchurch and passengers were taken by omnibus to their destination. It soon became apparent that a station was needed in in the town and eventually a line was opened in November 1862 to provide for one.

20.   Lord Roberts being greeted at Christchurch station by the town clerk, John Druitt, *c.*1902. To the right of the podium is the mayor, Colonel Monckton and members of the town council. The visit celebrated Lord Roberts' return from the Boer War.

OPENING OF NEW TRAMWAY AT CHRISTCHURCH

1a.   Specially decorated trams in a procession to mark the first day of operation on 17 October 1905. On the balcony of the Town Hall is Miss Ricardo of Bure Homage, a major Christchurch landowner, who rode in the first car.

County Borough of Bournemouth.

Opening of
Tramways to Christchurch

17th October, 1905.

Programme of Proceedings.

The Members of the Councils of Bournemouth, Branksome, Christchurch and Poole, and invited Officials (with Ladies) will assemble in the Square, Bournemouth, at 1.30 p.m., and mount cars (decorated suitably to the occasion) which, after being photographed, will proceed to Christchurch.

The Mayors and Town Clerks and the Chairman and Clerk of Branksome Council and the Chairman of the several Tramway Committees (and Ladies) are requested to take seats in the first car. Other cars are not reserved, but it is hoped that members of the several Tramway Committees (and Ladies) will ride in the second car as far as accommodation permits.

At Tuckton Bridge (the boundary of the Boroughs of Bournemouth and Christchurch) the occupants of the first car only will alight, when the Mayor of Christchurch (Lieut.-Col. Monckton, J.P.) will say a few words of welcome to the Borough of Christchurch.

1b.   Programme of Proceedings for the opening of the tramway to Christchurch. The first trams started from Bournemouth and after a brief ceremony at Tuckton Bridge, which marked the boundary of the boroughs of Christchurch and Bournemouth, they carried on to their destination (the Town Hall) in Christchurch.

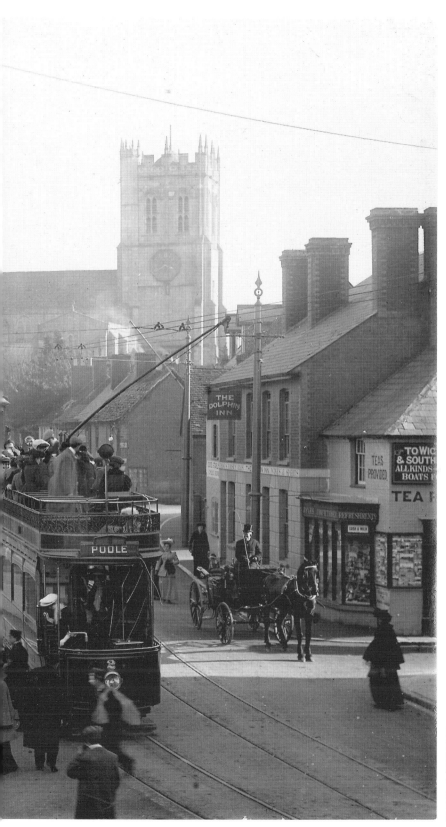

22. The Poole tram leaving the terminus in Church Street. The terminus was situated behind the *Dolphin Inn* yard, a sign for which can be seen on the right of the picture. The last tram and the first trolley bus ran through Christchurch on 8 April 1936.

23. An objection to proposals by Bournemouth Corporation to run trolley buses along Barrack Road. The original outcome of the objection is not known, although trolley buses were to run though the town for a number of years.

24. The first trolley bus to run from Bournemouth to Christchurch. This photograph was taken in Bournemouth, prior to making its first journey to Christchurch on Wednesday, 8 April 1936.

Local Industries

5.   Place Mill at the turn of the 20th century. There has been a mill on the site since Norman times. The mill is thought to have been a fulling mill in the 16th century, although it was more recently used to produce flour. It closed as a working mill in 1908 and was used as a boat shed for a number of years. Today it has been restored and has a small exhibition on the workings of a mill. The gentleman in the foreground is a fisherman and the small fishing boats were brought up to the quay by the mill for the off-loading of their catch.

26. Loading flour into a covered wagon at Knapp Mill. The Domesday Survey listed a mill on this site, valued at 20s. In the 16th century the building was a corn mill and it was later used as a fulling (wool cleaning) mill, being driven by water from the Avon. The original mill was destroyed in a fire in 1760 and was rebuilt by its owner Matthew Aldridge. Knapp Mill was demolished in 1921, shortly after being acquired by the West Hampshire Water Company.

27. The brewing staff of *Kings Brewery*, *c.*1860. In the foreground is William Miller, the foreman. The brewery was established by John King in 1723 and was one of a number situated in the High Street.

A wagon bound for Aldridge and ... who had a brewery next door to ... *Bow House* at the north end of the ...gh Street. The company was ...nded by George Olive Aldridge ... traded in the town for just over ... years until the turn of the 20th ...ntury.

FOLIO..........

Fordingbridge & Christchurch Breweries.

"*Manor of Burgate Moor* _____ 1895

Per Mr. Hammer.

Bot. of CHARLES ABSALOM,

MALTSTER AND BREWER.

ALE AND STOUT SUPPLIED IN SMALL CASKS.

Bass's Pale Ale and Guinness's Dublin Stout in Bottle.

Accounts Quarterly.   5 per cent. interest charged on overdue accounts.

6 oz   74 Tickets @ 6⁰   £1. 17 —

Paid 2/1/96

J.C.

A receipt, dated 1895, issued to ...Mr. Hammer by the Fordingbridge ...d Christchurch Breweries. In ...mmon with many towns, Christ-...urch had a number of breweries; ...s one was based just outside the ...wn, at Stanpit. These provided the ...al population with beer as the water ...pplies were often polluted. The ...ristchurch breweries have long ...ce disappeared.

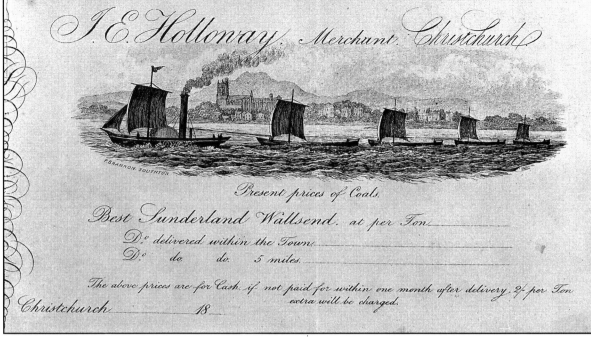

J.E. Holloway, Merchant, Christchurch

P. BRANNON. SOUTHTON.

Present prices of Coals.

Best Sunderland Wallsend. at per Ton _____

D.º delivered within the Town. _____

D.º   do.   do.   5 miles. _____

The above prices are for Cash. if not paid for within one month after delivery, 2/- per Ton extra will be charged.

Christchurch _____ 18 _____

30.   A printed notice for J.E. Holloway, with spaces for advisi on the cost of coal delivery. John Edward Holloway was architect and surveyor who lived in Barrack Road. The co was delivered to Christchurch by specially built steam tugs a barges which could negotiate the shallow waters of the harbou As well as delivering coal to the area, the family were al involved with ironstone mining at nearby Hengistbury Head

31.   An advertisement for Alfred Mallett, photographer, wh had premises in the High Street from 1881 until 1894 and the in Church Street, where he built a larger studio. He sold h business in 1904 to George Moss, another photographer, an moved to Tewkesbury. A number of the photographs in th book are the work of A. Mallett.

32a.   Edward Hart, a local taxidermist, who was based in the High Street. He learnt the trade from his father, William, who had diversified into fusee watch chain manufacture. In 1885, Edward opened a museum displaying mainly stuffed birds, some of which were very rare. Edward paid particular attention to detail when preparing the rarities, often placing them against a Christchurch background. Examples of Edward Hart's work may still be seen in the Red House Museum and Gardens.

32b.   An advertising card for Hart's museum. On the reverse an extract from *Bright's Guide to Bournemouth and Christchurch* reads: 'We should do our readers and visitors to Christchurch in general, a great injustice if we did not especially direct their attention to the Museum. Mr Hart has here a magnificent collection of British Birds, which we believe we are right in saying, is second to none in the Kingdom'.

VISITORS TO CHRISTCHURCH
SHOULD NOT FAIL SEEING
MR. HART'S
ORNITHOLOGICAL COLLECTION
OF OVER
One Thousand Specimens arranged in 300 Large Cases
AT HIS
MUSEUM, HIGH STREET.

" The Grotesque Groups are most curious and amusing, and far beyond any composition by Snyders or Hondekoeter, and almost worthy of a comparison with Landseer."—*Extract from Murray's Handbook.*

Open from 10 a.m. until 5 p.m.

2c.   Black-throated divers, rmerly on display in Hart's useum. Edward produced over)0 cases of stuffed birds and •me 200 still exist today. The ajority of Hart's collection are •ld by the Horniman Museum London, although 20 cases Edward's work are also held / the Hampshire County ›uncil Museums Service.

33.   A Burrell traction engine (works number 3363, registration AH081) owned by C. Light & Co Limited, who acquired it new in February 1914. C. Light & Co were timber merchants and owned sawing, planing and moulding mills at their premises in Bargates. The engine was later sold to T. Mossop and Co. Ltd. (see plate 34).

34.   A Foden steam lorry (works number 13494, registration OU 5864) built in 1930 and bought new by T. Mossop & Co. Limited, timber contractors.

35. Nurses from Christchurch Red Cross Hospital during the First World War. The building used for the hospital throughout the war was the workhouse in Fairmile. Afterwards the building reverted to its former purpose.

36. A card advertising a fund-raising event for the Red Cross hospital, dated 1917. Throughout the First World War, local generosity and the organisation of special events were needed to provide funds for nursing the wounded.

Christchurch Red Cross Hospital.

MRS. LASCELLES, of WICK HOUSE (near Wick Ferry) SOUTHBOURNE, is throwing open her Gardens on Wednesday, May 30th, & Thursday, May 31st, *1917* for the benefit of the above Hospital.

A rare JUDAS TREE, about 50ft. wide and 20ft. high, is in full bloom, and the largest MAIDENHAIR FERN TREE in the South of England, with other beautiful flowering shrubs, are to be seen.

Admission :—Wednesday 6d. ; Thursday, 1/-

Christchurch Hospital Carnival

Wednesday and Thursday
AUGUST 4th and 5th, 1937
in the
CENTRAL RECREATION GROUND
Admission each day, 6d.

and at

Town Hall, Christchurch, on
Wednesday evening, August 4th, doors open 8.30
and
Friday evening, August 6th, doors open 7.30

Official Programme

Issued by the Christchurch Hospital Association. **PRICE** 3D.

President : His Worship the Mayor of Christchurch (Alderman D. Galton, J.P.)
Chairman : Mr. D. Llewellyn
Hon. Treasurer : Mr. C. B. Hudson   Secretary : Alderman E. R. Oakley
Committee : The General Committee of the Christchurch
Hospital Association and co-opted members.

NOTICE, *re* The time table, list of events and order of proceedings.

The times stated will be adhered to as nearly as possible, but the Committee reserve the
right to alter, postpone, or vary the programme if found necessary owing to weather
conditions or any other causes.   E. Russell Oakley, *Secretary.*

Christchurch Times Ltd., 8 Bridge Street

---

2 to 3 p.m.—
JUDGING OF ALL COMPETITORS AND DISTRIBUTION
OF PRIZE CARDS.

3 p.m.—
CROWNING OF QUEEN OF THE CARNIVAL
by His Worship the Mayor of Christchurch (Alderman D. Galton,
J.P.)

Queen of the Carnival : Miss Queenie Newman, "Rose
Queen." Two Maids of Honour : Elsie Head and
Pamela Mortimer. Two Pages : Tommy Hatcher
and Freddy Warne, and Attendants. Tableau :
Decorated Floral.

The presentation of the Queen of the Carnival Tableau is by the
Townswomen's Guild (Christchurch Branch).

Costumes : Pale Pink Silk, Pale Blue and White.

The Carnival Procession will proceed to the Central Recreation
Ground from Clarendon Road via Portfield Road, Avenue
Road, Fairmile, Bargates, and High Street.
Chief Marshal—Mr. D. Llewellyn.

The Procession will be started by the Mayoress of Christchurch,
headed by the Town Band.

4 p.m.—
AT CENTRAL RECREATION GROUND (Admission 6d.)
Parade in the Arena of Prize-winning Competitors. Distribution
of Prizes by the Mayoress of Christchurch.

General announcements and information regarding the proceedings
will be made by Radio Loud Speaker.

4.30 p.m.—
Afternoon Performance in the Arena of the Celebrated
WIGHT RIDERS IN COSSACK AND GAUCHO
TRICK RIDING DISPLAY.

Twelve Isle of Wight Horsemen and Twelve Horses in Thrilling
Displays of Horsemanship, which include Lance and Sword
Pegging. Roman Riding. Roping and Trick Riding.

Seats in the Arena : Chairs 6d. Forms 3d.

5 p.m.—
TEA. Tent for Sale of Teas and Refreshments. Arranged by the
Ladies' Carnival Committee.

Minerals, Ice Cream, Fruit, Sweets on Sale in the Ground.

6 p.m.—
QUAINT DOG SHOW. Judges : Miss N. Woodifield, Mr. C. R.
Dickenson.

Open to all Dog Owners in the District.

Class 1.—Smallest Dog (over one year).
Class 2.—Fattest Dog (any age).
Class 3.—Dog with most spots.
Class 4.—Dog with longest tail.
Class 5.—Dog with longest beg (no tit-bits allowed).
Class 6.—Dogs' Fancy Dress Parade.
Class 7.—Dog with prettiest owner. Lady or gent, boy
or girl.
Class 8.—Tail Waggers Class. Speed trial for fast tail
wagging.

For Rules and Prize Money see Schedule.
Admission to Dog Show Enclosure 3d. Judging will commence at
6 p.m.

6.30 p.m.—
THE MUDEFORD SUNSHINE GIRLS. Tap Dancers and Dance
Display.

7 p.m.—
ENGLISH FOLK DANCE SOCIETY. Display by members of
"The New Milton Folk Dance Centre" and "The Foresters'
Morris Club," including Winkaton Sword Dance, Morris Dances,
Country Dances, "Christchurch Bells," "Parson's Farewell,"
"Nonsuch," and others.

HAM COMPETITION on Ground. For particulars see Thursday
programme.

8 p.m.—
Evening Performance of WIGHT RIDERS in the Arena. Trick
Riding Display by Twelve Isle of Wight Horsemen and Horses,
including Lance and Sword Pegging, Roman Riding and Trick
Riding. Seats in the Arena : Chairs 6d. Forms 3d.

8.30 p.m.—
OPEN AIR DANCE. Enclosure on Ground.

9 to 1 a.m.—
At the Town Hall. GRAND CARNIVAL DANCE. Doors open
8.30. Admission Ticket 2/-. On Sale or at Door. M.C. : Mr.
J. W. Trevis. Dance Band : Mr. J. Elmes.

Note.—Old English Fair, Roundabouts, Swings and several of the
latest mechanical amusements will be on the ground as in
previous years.

---

37. Selection of pages from the programme for Christchurch hospital carnival, held in 1937. Many hospitals relied on funds raised through carnivals. Events held during this carnival were a procession of floats and people in fancy dress (11 different classes), a *Cossack* and *Gaucho* riding display, a dog show, dancing, a children's procession and 'the trial for the Twynham flitch'—a mock trial whereby applicants had to present a case for the custody of the 'flitch' or side of bacon.

38. Gardeners in the grounds of the Red House, by now a private house, probably belonging to the Rev. Bush, Vicar of Christchurch. The building was originally the parish poorhouse and later became a workhouse. Inmates earned their keep by knitting stockings and making fusee watch chains, both thriving industries in Christchurch at the time. The photograph shows part of what is now the south garden (formerly an area for drying laundry) and in the background is the well of the original workhouse.

39. A table, piled high with bread. This formed part of Elliott's Charity, whereby bread was distributed in the priory on the second Sunday of every month. There were about fifty recipients of the loaves which were paid for by money left in the 1677 will of Edward Elliott.

40. An advertisement for Christchurch school, a boarding school for boys, which was run by Josiah Evans. The school, established in 1827, was just outside the town, in Purewell.

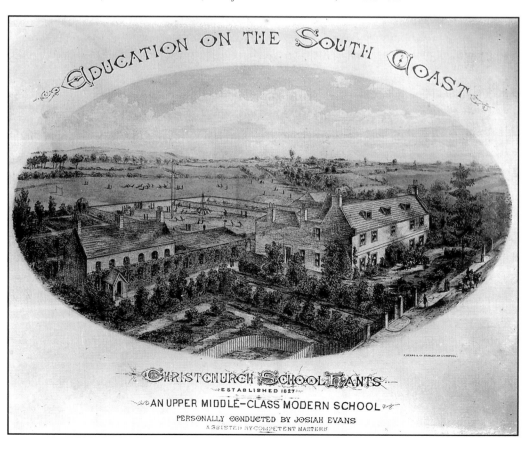

EDUCATION ON THE SOUTH COAST

CHRISTCHURCH SCHOOL HANTS
ESTABLISHED 1827
AN UPPER MIDDLE-CLASS MODERN SCHOOL
PERSONALLY CONDUCTED BY JOSIAH EVANS
ASSISTED BY COMPETENT MASTERS

41. Pupils and school masters of Christchurch school, *c.*1878. Also in the photograph are three 'ordinary bicycles', which were more popularly known as penny-farthings. These were still a relatively new invention at the time.

42. Christchurch school football team for the years 1892-3.

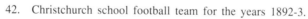

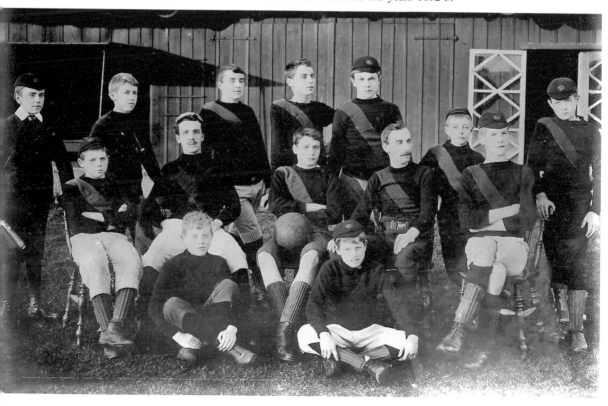

43.   Staff and pupils from the Congregational school (also known as the Independent school), dressed in costume for a school play. They are standing in front of the Congregational (now the United Reformed) church, in what is today part of Saxon Square.

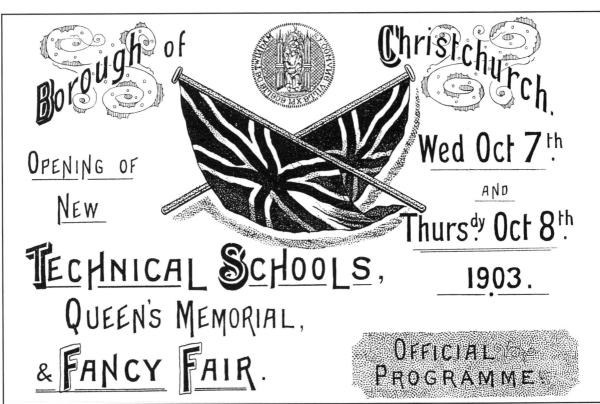

Borough of Christchurch.

Opening of New Technical Schools, Queen's Memorial, & Fancy Fair.

Wed Oct 7th
and
Thursdy Oct 8th
1903.

Official Programme

44.   The front of the official programme produced to mark the opening of the new Technical Schools in October 1903. The opening ceremony was carried out by the Right Honourable Lord Lieutenant of Hampshire, Earl Northbrook, who unveiled a memorial medallion of the late Queen Victoria. The school was inaugurated in 1898 and classes were held in various buildings throughout the town until additions were made to the Town Hall building to provide classrooms. Among the subjects taught were art, needlework, science, wood carving, mathematics, book keeping and languages.

45.   Members of Christchurch Adult School and Institute, which was based in Millhams Street. Four of the members have been identified as Herbert Druitt and D. Lane (back row, second from left and fifth from left respectively), Mr. Owen and William Aldridge (second row, fourth from right and sixth from right). The photograph is dated June 1914.

6.   The Square House, formerly on the junction of Wick Lane and the High Street, *c*.1840. This Palladian-style edifice vas built *c*.1776 by John Cook, a local brewer and five times mayor of Christchurch. The building was pulled down in 1958 nd today the site is an arcade of shops and a post office.

47.   Junction of the High Street in the snow, *c.*1910. On the left is 3 High Street, George Ferrey & Son. On the right, at the junction with Castle Street, is Taylor's Creamery Tea Room. The building was the Assembly Rooms for a few years and also provided accommodation for the *George Inn*.

48.   A view looking north along the High Street, *c*.1900. The far end of the High Street is very different today as the two buildings that can just be seen in the background have since been demolished. On the left, in the foreground, is a shop established by George Ferrey, a milliner and draper. Other shops that can just be made out on the right are Hayward (watchmaker) and G.E. Loveless (baker and confectioner). The premises of W. Hayward also doubled as a registry office for servants. An early car can just be made out on the road.

49.   G. Ferrey & Son, decorated for the coronation of Edward VII, 1902. George Ferrey was a tailor who lived and worked at the draper's store in the High Street. The building was known as Clingan House, after John Clingan, a 17th-century mercer (a dealer in textiles), who established Clingan's Charity. The Ferrey family traded in the High Street from 1816 until 1936.

50.   The High Street premises of Benjamin Joy Tucker, saddler, in November 1937. B.J. Tucker took over the premises from another saddler (John and Lucy Lemmon) in 1872. This long established firm eventually closed down in October 1938.

51.   Advertisements for Ferrey & Son and B.J. Tucker, taken from *Tucker's Christchurch Almanack* for 1893. These give an idea of the variety of goods sold by both firms.

2. A garage for storing cars and cycles and a bookshop run by Russell Oakley, *c*.1930. The premises were situated at 9 High Street. Cars had become a regular feature in the streets of Christchurch and there are no fewer than 12 car engineers, garages and proprietors listed in the directory for this date. Russell Oakley was a councillor for Central and Jumpers Ward, founder member (with Herbert Druitt) of the Christchurch Historical Society, and a local historian who wrote several books on the town, including one on smuggling.

53.   'Shaws House', 20 High Street, *c*.1904. This late Tudor building was pulled down in 1914 to make way for the post office. On the left is Crowley and Son Ltd., wine merchants and on the right is Cuff (water) miller and corn merchant. A sign on the first floor notes that the building had been sold by H.A. Woof, estate agents, auctioneer and valuer. H.A. Woof was based in a building on the other side of Crowley and Son Ltd.

54 .   End of the High Street, *c*.1905. The four men in front of *The Antelope Hotel* are standing next to the drinking fountain which gave the site the name *Fountain Corner*. The fountain was relocated with the building of the by-pass and a traffic island (still known as the *Fountain Roundabout*) built in its place. The building on the right of the photograph is Frisby's the boot maker at 32 High Street. Beyond the Frisby's signs are two others that bear the legend 'Agent for Achille Serre High Class Dyer and Cleaner London'.

55.   End of High Street, 1938. More cars are in evidence and a garage can be seen on the left of the picture. The tracks for the trams disappeared two years earlier, but the overhead cables of the still relatively new trolley buses are in evidence. The building in the centre served a dual purpose. 'Francis' was a ladies' outfitters and the initials ARP (Air Raid Patrol) show the other role of the building and act as a reminder that the Second World War had started. The ARP officer was Captain Victor D. Smith.

56. William James Payn and F.E. Williams, two stores at the north end of the High Street, on the east side, *c*.1885. Payn's shop was a linen drapers and outfitters in a building known as Manchester House. This building was pulled down in the 1960s and was replaced by Barclays bank. Williams' was a grocer's shop from 1845-94. During the First World War the building was used by service men as a Union Jack Club, a meeting place where refreshments were served. This building and the one to the right of it were pulled down to make way for the new shops in Saxon Square.

57. Christchurch High Street, *c*.1910. Public transport in the form of a tram and a horse and carriage are evident; otherwise the street is almost empty. The plain Georgian-style building on the right is Druitt House. It was built by James Druitt (1816-1904) who was five times mayor of Christchurch, a town clerk and Justice of the Peace. The house remained in the family until his son, Herbert, left the house and his collection of books, documents and artifacts to the town. Today it is the library. A small sign beyond Druitt House is that of Henry Edward Holloway, hairdresser at no.14 and beyond that, at no.10, is A. and L. Lovett, stationers. On the other side of the road is Froud Brothers, outfitters.

8. The east side of the High Street, *c*.1875. On the corner is the boot and shoe warehouse of Samuel Savage, the shoemaker. Rows of shoes and boots can just be made out in the window. Next door is the *Ship Inn* and the building to the right of the public house is the former home of Robert Harvey Cox, one of three fusee watch chain manufacturers in Christchurch in the 19th century. The building next door was a Protestant Dissenters school, which was run by John Saunders and Mary Young in the first half of the 19th century.

9. Looking south along the High Street towards Church Street, *c*.1920. On the left is the London and Central Meat Company Limited, with a sign below which says 'Prime Canterbury Lamb'. The tobacconist's next door, run by James Williams, also shared premises with the lending library. The shop further along, with the elaborate railing, was that of William Tucker and Son.

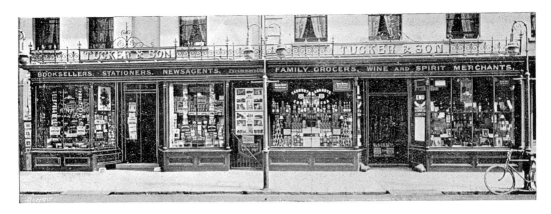

W. Tucker & Son, 52, High St., Christchurch

Established	Tea & Coffee Specialists, Booksellers and Stationers	Telephone
1798.	High-class Groceries & Provisions, Wines & Spirits.	4 x.

60. W. Tucker and Son, 1909. This large store, which sold a great variety of food, household objects and stationery, was established by Ambrose Tucker in 1798. The firm offered a range of services, including customer accounts and a delivery service within the town, as well as to Mudeford, Southbourne and other villages in the neighbourhood. The stationery side of the firm also produced a yearly *Tuckers' Christchurch Almanack*. The shop eventually closed in 1958.

61. The United Reformed church, formerly known as the Congregational church, in Millhams Street, just off the High Street. It was designed by W. Stint of Warminster. To cope with the ever increasing congregation, the old church was pulled down in 1866 and the present one built in its place. In 1960, the church celebrated 300 years of worship in the town.

Castle Street, Bridge Street and Rotten Row

62.   Castle Street, 1881. This snowy scene started as a blizzard in January, making access to the town almost impossible. The roads were blocked and the rivers frozen over. It was not until March that the snow finally disappeared.

63.   A similar view of Castle Street, *c.*1895, showing the buildings a little more clearly than the previous photograph. On the left is the Wiltshire and Dorset bank, built on the site of the *White Hart* public house. Today it is Lloyds bank. Further along, above the horse and carriage, is a sign for *Caines Hotel*. This was a temperance hotel run by Mrs. Anna Caines.

64.   Today this building is known as the Old Court House and houses the New Forest Perfumery. It was actually a building
demolished in 1884 and rebuilt to the right (the shop with writing in the window 'Riding Breeches, Livery') that was the
original Court House.

N.S. NEWLYN'S FAMILY HOTEL.

POST HORSES & MODERN BUILT CARRIAGES. *CHRISTCHURCH, HANTS.* **AGENT TO THE S.W. RAILWAY COMPANY.**

IMPORTER & DEALER IN FOREIGN WINES & SPIRITS.

An Omnibus serves all the Trains f.m London for Bournemouth except the 5.10 P.M.Tr.n f.m Waterloo. Also Omnibuses f.m every T.n to the Kings Arms.

SEE ADVERTISEMENT AT THE END OF BOOK.

5. *Newlyn's Family Hotel*, now known as the *King's Arms Hotel*. It was built in 1801 by George Rose, M.P. for Christchurch and sold to Nicholas Sambrook Newlyn, *c.*1857.

6. Castle Street, 1830. This postcard shows the confusion that often arises over the start and end of the streets. Castle Street begins at the other side of the bridge, by the railings. At the end of Castle Street the old Town Hall can be seen on its former site. The bridge illustrated in the sketch is the old medieval town bridge which still stands.

Bridge St. Ch. ch.

67.   A flood in Bridge Street, 1 January 1915, looking towards the town. The bridge in the photograph is known as the
Waterloo Bridge and was built by William Hiscock in 1817. The building that can just be seen over the bridge, on the left,
was a former home and studio of Arthur Romney Green, a nationally renowned furniture maker and woodcarver in the early
20th century.

8.   Looking towards Bridge Street from the Convent Walk. The Avon is on the right, while on the left is the mill stream which is crossed by the Mill Stream Bridge (also known as Mews Bridge and Millhams Bridge). The house almost in the centre of the photograph is still known as Quartley's after the doctor and surgeon who lived there. The building on the right of Quartley's was taken down when the bridge was widened.

9.   The Town Bridge, the only one of three bridges built in the medieval period to survive today. It was widened in 1899 to cope with the increase in traffic. For a while the bridge was known as Quartley's Bridge, after Dr. Arthur Quartley, a mayor of Christchurch, who also had a reluctant involvement with smugglers.

70. A view looking along almost the whole length of Bridge Street towards the town, *c*.1900. Preston's on the left was run by John Preston, who is listed in directories as a stone and marble mason, but diversified into a number of other areas. Preston's were in Bridge Street for just over 50 years.

ESTABLISHED 1863.

ESTABLISHED 1863.

JOHN PRESTON

JOHN PRESTON,

The Christchurch Monumental Works,

AVON WHARF, CHRISTCHURCH.

COAL, COKE, FIREWOOD, BRICK, SLATE, AND TIMBER MERCHANT.
Sole Agent for the Best Old Round Wood Hand-picked Yorkshire Coals.

THE ANGLO-BAVARIAN BREWERY Co.'s ALES AND STOUT
In 4½, 9, and 18 Gallon Casks.
Also in Screw-stoppered Bottles, at 2/6 and 3/- per dozen Imperial Pints.

Garden Edgings, Flower Pots, and Vases. Wheelbarrows and Ladders.

ALL KINDS OF BUILDING MATERIALS KEPT IN STOCK.
Marquees, Tents, Tables, and Chairs for Sale and Hire.

CABINET MAKER, UPHOLSTERER & UNDERTAKER
FURNITURE AND BEDDING WAREHOUSE.

WORKMEN SENT OUT.   **REMOVALS TO ALL PARTS.**

Agent for the Anglo-Bavarian Ales and Stout, and Atlas Fire and Life Assurance Company.

71. An advertisement for John Preston of Bridge Street, showing the variety of trades covered by the company.

2. Christchurch post office at Bridge Street, before it was moved to the High Street in 1914. The post office was run by members of the Pike family for a number of years. Today Christchurch post office is in an arcade of shops on the site of the former Square House.

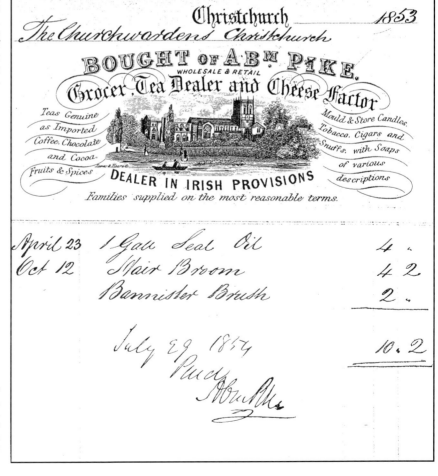

Christchurch _____ 1853

The Churchwardens Christchurch

BOUGHT of AB^m PIKE.
WHOLESALE & RETAIL

Grocer, Tea Dealer and Cheese Factor

Teas Genuine as Imported Coffee, Chocolate and Cocoa. Fruits & Spices

Mould & Store Candles. Tobacco, Cigars and Snuffs. with Soaps of various descriptions

DEALER IN IRISH PROVISIONS

Families supplied on the most reasonable terms.

April 23	1 Gall Seal Oil	4	.
Oct 12	Hair Broom	4	2
	Bannister Brush	2	.
	July 29 1854	10	2

3. A billhead, made out to the churchwardens of Christchurch, dated 1853 and paid in July 1854. Abraham Pike, who issued the billhead, had a grocer's shop in Bridge Street and also ran the post office.

74. Major Edric Sidney Martin, MRCVS, out and about in his car. Major Martin was the town vet and meat inspector until the 1930s and lived at Magnolia House in Rotten Row.

75. Magnolia House was the home of the Goddard family for a number of years. They lived and worked in the Christchurch area from the early 1870s onwards. John Bedloe Goddard was born in November 1838, the only son of Eliza and John Bryer Goddard, a surgeon. He became a well respected water colour landscape painter, exhibiting regularly in London and the provinces. His two sisters were also prominent local artists. Amelia (1847-1928) specialised in New Forest and Gypsy subjects, while Eliza (1840-1915) painted flowers. They continued to live at Magnolia House until 1907, when they moved to Thorney Hill, Bransgore.

76.   An area that was formerly known as Rotten Row, possibly a corruption of *route du roi* or *Royal Route* and a reminder that Christchurch was once a rotten borough. Rotten Row was just east of the Waterloo Bridge in Bridge Street. This photograph is dated *c.*1875.

OPENING OF CONVENT WALK - MAYORESS PLANTING CORONATION OAK

77.   The opening of Convent Walk to the public, during the coronation celebrations of George V in 1911. An oak sapling was planted to mark the occasion by the mayoress, Mrs. Robert Druitt, who is almost hidden in this photograph.

78.   Convent Walk, looking towards the Constable's House and Quartley's House. The term 'convent' initially applied to religious orders of either monks (as in the case of Christchurch) or nuns. The walk was originally used by the canons for contemplation.

9.   Local boys and men on the frozen mill stream, Christmas Day, 1890. There were a number of hard frosts in the last alf of the 19th century and this was one of the more severe winters recollected by William Tucker in his reminiscences. he mill stream is normally a fast flowing stretch of water.

80.   A view of Church Street taken just before the trams came into operation. The presence of George Moss's shop on the left dates the photograph to c.1904-5. George Moss, photographer, took over the Priory Studio from Alfred Mallet in 1904. On the left are the premises of E.J. and C. Burry. An interesting feature of the photograph is the use of barrels for supporting scaffolding.

81. Church Street after a late snow storm which fell in Christchurch on 25 April 1908. By this tim
trams had been in operation for about two and a half years. Although electricity was available ar

supplied the trams, many streets in Christchurch continued to use gas for street lighting until the 1930s. A gas lamp can be seen on the left of the picture in front of Lane's the grocer's.

82. The *Dolphin Inn*, Church Street, *c*.1930. The original inn was destroyed by a fire in December 1864 and was rebuilt a few years later. When trams started running in 1905, the *Dolphin* yard became the tram depot and later it housed the trolley bus turntable. The building no longer exists as it was pulled down in 1973 and replaced by shops and offices.

83. The *Eight Bells*, Church Street, *c*.1907. This former public house was one of the smuggling haunts in Christchurch. Legend relates that there was a tunnel leading from the basement to the *Ship in Distress* at Stanpit. The gentleman standing outside is Arthur Joy, the last landlord. Today the building is a gift shop and still bears its old name. To the right of the photograph is the Priory Tea House.

74. A view of the far end of Church Street, looking north, c.1895. The two gentlemen in conversation are Mr. Woodwark of Church Street and Mr. Tours, a coachman.

75. Church Street, c.1905. The building on the right is Church Hatch. An interesting feature of the house is the arrangement of mathematical tiles which face the back of it. One 18th-century occupant was Mrs. Perkins, who had a fear of being buried alive. On her death she was buried in a coffin rigged to a system of flags that could be raised if she remained alive. Her mausoleum can still be seen close to the castle. On the left is a row of three medieval houses.

86.   The junction of Church Lane and Quay Road, looking towards Church Street. The buildings on either side of the lane have changed very little since this photograph was taken *c.*1890. The traffic, however, has increased as the lane is on a one-way system.

87.   Wick Lane in flood at the turn of the 20th century. This lane leads to Wick Ferry, which took passengers across to the Bournemouth side of the river Stour. On the left, where two people can be seen peering out of the building, is the Priory School.

88.   Another snowy scene, this time of Quay Road. On the left is the former workhouse, now the Red House Museum. The building took its name from the colour of its bricks. On the right is the vicarage. Just behind the wall, next to the vicarage, is the churchyard of the priory.

89. Looking north along Quay Road. This photograph was taken from what is now a car park which leads to the quay and Place Mill.

The Priory

0. Christchurch Priory with fishing nets in the foreground. For many years salmon fishing was an important occupation n the town and fish were caught at the mouth of the harbour. Today salmon fishing is a recreational activity and stretches f the rivers are owned by private fisheries.

91. A view of the priory showing its proximity to the quay. In the foreground are Place Mill and the sailing club.

92. Kaiser Wilhelm II leaving Christchurch Priory after a morning service on 1 December 1907. The kaiser was a frequent visitor to nearby Highcliffe Castle.

93. Priory church bell-ringers. The campanologists are (back row, left to right): S. Best, G. Preston, H. Best, W. Saffery; (front row): E. Walters, R. Hinton, H. Bagshott, G. Vey.

94. The priory church choir of 1890. The choristers are (back row, right to left): Alfred Mallet, Charles Burry, Belton, Henry Bagshot, Rev. T.H. Bush, James Druitt, T. Brown, J. Goater; (second row): E. Macklin, J. Hyde, Frederick Stainer, Andrew Lane, Alan Druitt, C. Croucher, C. Miller; (third row): George Ferrey, H. Galton, W. Early, Marshall, E. Upshall, G. Burt, G. Galton, A. Vick, Bates, J.B. Jenkins; (front row): Hopkins, G. Watton, J. Preston-Hayward, P. Davis.

95.   A view of the west tower surrounded by scaffolding during work of 1906. The weather vane, which can just be discerned, has a traditional place in the smuggling history of Christchurch. Look-outs in the tower would turn the vane to indicate to their fellow smugglers the direction from which the customs officers were approaching.

96.   Restoration of the south nave aisle in 1906. The work was carried out by G. Tompson of Peterborough.

97.   A stone coffin found on the south side of the choir aisle during the restoration work of 1906.

98. Re-flooring the nave after first pulling out the old pews of 1841. The new floor comprised six inches of concrete and one inch of fine cement, with wooden blocks on top. The work, carried out in 1912, was undertaken by Tompson of Peterborough and the architect was Sir G. Jackson, R.A.

99.   Restoration work carried out in 1912. Standing on the left is James T. Hyde, the parish clerk, and on the right is Herbert E. Miller, the verger.

0.   An early labour-saving device for cutting grass! The large building in the background is Priory House which is on
e site of the ancient priory. It was partly rebuilt and converted by Gustavus Brander, an antiquarian and curator of the
itish Museum, in 1776. In 1807, it was the home of Louis Philippe, Duke of Orleans during his exile.

Christchurch Quay

101. The quay, showing (from left to right) the coal warehouse, Place Mill and the club house of Christchurch Sailing Club, *c.*1900. The sailing club was established in 1883. In the 1960s the building was replaced by a new club house.

102. Christchurch Quay, showing the shelter, priory and Place Mill. The shelter no longer exists, although a bandstand was built close by in the 1930s. The bandstand was donated ('anonymously') by the general manager of the West Hampshire Water Company, David Llewellyn.

46394. CHRISTCHURCH, PRIORY & SHELTER.

103. Quay Meadow, which was by the quay, at the turn of the 20th century. The buildings in the centre background are the National Schools in Wick Lane, now known as the Priory School. Most of the area has now been developed into a housing estate.

104. *Ye Wagon & Horses, c.1900.* On the left of the picture, Bemister's Fountain can just be made out in front of Hodges and Mason, cycle makers. The public house was replaced by the *Fountain Hotel, c.1907.* Both buildings stood at the north end of the High Street, in approximately the position of the present-day roundabout.

105.   The *Cross Keys* public house at 32 Barrack Road, *c*.1910. By the 1920s it had stopped trading as a public house and ad become the premises of Messrs. Miller, undertakers and builders.

106.   Barrack Road at the end of the 19th century. The road was named after Christchurch barracks and was a small track efore they were built. The road has since been widened and the trees lining the road cut down.

107.   Fountain Corner, at the junction of the High Street, Barrack Road and Bargates, on 10 February 1937. This view is looking west along Barrack Road. Fountain Corner is so called after the fountain that can be seen next to the bollard on the right. The fountain and drinking trough were erected in memory of Samuel Bemister who was seven times mayor of Christchurch. The fountain now stands at the corner of Wick Lane and Whitehall.

108.   The junction of Barrack Road with Stour Road, *c*.1925. In the background near the railway bridge, railway signals for Christchurch station can just be made out. On the left-hand side of the road is a hay wagon.

109.   Looking east along Jumpers Road, from Barrack Road, *c*.1920. On the right is St George's Mission church, also known as the 'tin church' after the materials used in its construction. The area is named after the Jumper family who held the estate.

110. A sketch of what is thought to be the old Bargate, a gate in the defensive wall of the town, built c.901. The moveable gate was repaired in 1728 and was eventually removed in 174 by the mayor, Thomas Jeans. The Bargate was situated between the *Green Tree Inn* and Aldridge's Brewery at the north end of the High Street.

111. Looking north along Bargates towards the now removed signal box of Christ church station, c.1900. On the left of the picture is the Bargate post office, which was a sub office of the town. The sub postmaster at this time was J. Morris. Apart from the absence of vehicles, the road has only changed superficially.

112. Pound Lane as seen from Bargates, c.1950. The brick wall on the left was the town pound in which stray cattle and horses were kept.

113a. The old *Red Lion*, Bargates, *c.*1900. The licensee at the time, who is listed as a beer retailer, was George Budden.

113b. Demolition of the old *Red Lion* in 1904-5. The public house was pulled down and rebuilt further back when the road was widened to make way for the passage of the trams.

4. A view of part of Bargates from Beaconsfield Road, 1900. The cob and thatch cottage on the left was known as *uonymus* (the name can just be made out between the upstairs windows) and was pulled down only hours before a eservation order was placed on it in 1971.

5. Old Pit, Bargates, *c*.1890. e small thatched cottage on e right was occupied by illiam Clark, the chimney eep. On the left, the part of e house just visible was owned Tom Barrows, while the shop the centre was run by Mary n Farwell. Mrs. Farwell was beer retailer and shopkeeper d a row of bottles can be seen the window. Her father ran *Horse and Groom* public use, which was also in rgates, opposite Silver Street.

116. Pit, at the back of what was Spicer Street, 31 January 1937. This area took its name from the gravel pit on which it was built. The building and the opening of the by-pass in 1958 led to the demolition of Pit, Pound Lane and Spicer Street.

117. Henry Brown and Son, butcher's shop, Bargates, c.1895. The absence of chilled cabinets and refrigerators meant that food had to be hung outside to be kept cool. The business was taken over by Charles Brown, c.1900.

18. Trim and Fosters, grocer's, *c.*1935. The shop, at 9 Bargates, was next door to the *Duke of Wellington* public house. Judging by the contents in the window, the shop sold jewellery, toys and buttons in addition to grocery, sweets, cigarettes and tobacco.

119.   The neocassical Georgian House (centre) which was built in the 17th century and was pulled down in 1956 to make way for the by-pass. Former occupants included Walter Gould, who was thought, by some, to be the richest man in Christchurch, and Theo Brown, the jeweller who later became the assistant verger at the priory. To the left of the Georgian House is L.F. Thompson & Sons Ltd., 'cash butchers', and to the right is a general store and confectioner's. The photograph is dated *c.*1937.

120.   A view of West End which was a continuation of Bargates, *c.*1880. In the foreground is Joseph Brewer, the town scavenger. He paid for the privilege of collecting sweepings from the road, which he piled onto his donkey-drawn cart. He also watered the streets, which were little more than dirt tracks, to keep down the dust. He was paid for this service by the local shopkeepers.

21.   Looking north along Fairmile, *c*.1900. The cottage on the right is typical of the cob (a mixture of clay and straw) and thatch cottages that used to line the road. These have since disappeared and the road has been widened.

22.   Grove Lane (east end), *c*.1900. This leafy road off Fairmile is now known as Grove Road East and is a built-up area. The signpost at the end of the lane is in Fairmile and turning right would take the traveller into Christchurch.

123.   The official opening of the Drill Hall in Portfield Road. The Drill Hall was used by the Hampshire Regiment, 5th/7th Battalion (Territorial Army). The area known as Portfield Road used to be farmed in the strip cultivated system that was common in Britain until the Enclosure Acts. Portfield was enclosed in 1873, which released land on which to build, and led to the expansion of the town. In addition 10 acres of the land were allocated for use as a recreation ground.

FAIRFIELD CHRISTCHURCH

24.   Fairfield, built on farm land formerly owned by the Earl of Malmesbury. Both Fairmile and Fairfield take their name .om the town fairs that used to be held there. Christchurch had two fairs: the older was the 'Priory Fair' which was held Trinity Sunday. It was established by Richard de Redvers and belonged to the Lord of the Manor of Christchurch vynham. The other was 'St Faith's Fair', named after the day on which it was held. This was also known as the 'Borough ir' as it was owned by the Lord of the Manor of the Borough.

125.   Christchurch barracks with the river Stour in the foreground. The barracks were built in the 1790s to house soldiers stationed there in the event of an invasion by the French. Another purpose of the barracks was to house the light dragoons, who assisted the excise officers in thwarting smuggling activities. When they were built, the barracks stood almost in isolation along a track. The track is now Barrack Road, a busy thoroughfare.

126.   The 4th Voluntary Battery Hampshire Rifle Corps, B. Company, Christchurch on camp at Holmsley in the New Forest. The men in the photograph are (from left to right): Private Martin, Sergeant Brookes, Private Watcher, Private Stevens, Private Shelton, Private Burry, Private E. Haywood, Private E. Morris. In the front row are (kneeling): Private Snooks, Private A. Troke and Captain Wagg. The photograph was taken by Corporal H.E. Miller, verger of Christchurch Priory.

27.   Indian Troops and Kitchener with the doctor from Barton Camp (fifth from the left), outside the priory in 1915.
Wounded Indian troops were housed at a rest area in New Milton which was close to the Indian military depot at Milford
on Sea.

128.   Wounded soldiers at the Union Jack Club celebrating the Christmas festivities in 1915. The club was set up during the First World War in the High Street and one of its mainstays was Herbert Druitt who, with his sister Charlotte, would take mince pies and oranges to the troops on Christmas Day.

129.   The South Africa Ward at Christchurch Hospital, decorated for Christmas, December 1915. Some of the soldier have been identified as (from the left, clockwise): Wilson, Dilworth, Derrick, Emmerson, Eldred, Broad, Rose, Barlow and Burgess.

130. A party of wounded soldiers from Boscombe Military Hospital, October 1918. The photograph was taken by H.E. Miller outside the North Porch.

131. A temporary bridge built over the Stour by the Royal Engineers. The Experimental Bridging Company of the Royal Engineers was formed in Christchurch shortly after the First World War, with the appointment of Major Martel.

Thanksgiving Week.

CHRISTCHURCH AND DISTRICT
WAR SAVINGS COMMITTEE.

THE GUN will be met on TUESDAY, November 19th, instead of Monday, as previously advertised.

THE PROCESSION will be as follows, leaving the Railway Station at 10.0 a.m. :--

BAND OF NEW ZEALAND ENGINEERS
(by kind permission of Col. G. Barclay, V.D).

TROOPS.

W.A.A.C.'s.

SCOUTS.

THE GUN.

MAYOR & CORPORATION with MILITARY OFFICERS and others.

ROUTE :--

From Railway Station, Stour Road, to Barrack Road over Railway Bridge to Cemetery Corner — Fairmile — Bargates — Town Hall (Halt for ADDRESS and NATIONAL ANTHEM), after which proceed to Mudeford—Gun to halt at Pillar Box and Troops dismiss.

The Gun and Band will then visit Highcliffe and Hinton.

Printed at the " Christchurch Times " Offices, Bridge Street.

132a. Christchurch and district War Savings Committee Gun Campaign, 1918, showing the gun breech and limber. The campaign, a national initiative, was set up to raise money for the purchase of guns—'the greater the Gun Power, the sooner the War will end in final Victory'. A large gun left Christchurch station on 19 November and was paraded through the streets of Christchurch to mark the start of a week of campaigning and collecting. A total of £27,000 was collected for war bonds and certificates in the borough.

132b. A handbill detailing the route of the gun and advising of a change in the date.

3. A certificate awarded to Stanley Walter White of [S]our Road during the Recreation Fund presentations on [ ] August 1919. Speeches were made and certificates of [ho]nour and medals presented to those who had served in [the] First World War. The awards were handed out by the [M]ayor of Christchurch, Robert Druitt.

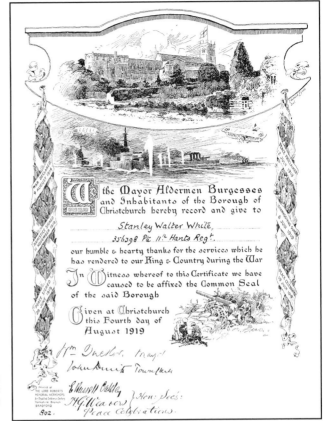

4. The police station in Stour Road, sandbagged against [po]tential bomb damage during the Second World War. The [tre]es and trolley bus poles have been painted with white [str]ipes so that they can be spotted during the blackout.

Special Events

135.   The passing of the first Parliamentary Reform Act in 1832. To ensure that there were enough votes under this new
Act to entitle the town to a Member of Parliament, the boundaries of the borough were extended. These new boundaries
went from Muscliff to Hinton and northwards to include Thorney Hill and Hurn. The Act was celebrated by a dinner, with
three rows of tables, holding between 300 and 400 dishes, which stretched the length of the High Street.

136.   A parade through the town to celebrate the marriage of King George V and Queen Mary (as they became known)
on 6 July 1883. Matilda Jane Druitt, who lived in the large house on the right, wrote in her diary for the day: 'The house
was decorated for the wedding of Princess Mary of Teck with Prince George, Duke of York. Went to the recreation ground
to see the illuminations'.

37. Druitt House decorated for an event, probably Queen Victoria's Diamond Jubilee, in 1897. The house, owned by James Druitt and his family, was always decorated for special events. Events that were held during the festivities included illuminations and a procession followed by fireworks.

38. A memorial service held in the priory in honour of the late Queen Victoria. The service was attended by the mayor, William Tucker, the corporation and a large congregation. The initial 'V' can be made out in flowers.

139. Proclamation of the accession of King Edward VII being announced from the balcony of the Town Hall by the mayor William Tucker. Among the people on the balcony are the mace-bearer, Sir George Meyrick and the Sheriff of the County.

Coronation of
T.M. King George V. & Queen Mary

JUNE, 1911.

CHRISTCHURCH
        CELEBRATION.

Mayor—Robert Druitt, Esq., J.P.

Dear Sir,

A Meeting of the Decorations

Committee will be held in the Council Chamber,

Town Hall, on Monday Evening,

March 13th 1911, at Eight o'clock, when

your attendance is requested.

Yours faithfully,

W. E. MOOREY,

Secretary.

140. An invitation to Melville Druitt, requesting his presence a a meeting of the Decorations Committee. The committee was on of a number set up in Christchurch to plan the coronation of Kin George V and Queen Mary. The mayor of Christchurch at the tim was Melville Druitt's brother.

141a. Festivities celebrating the Coronation of King George V, 1911, showing the carnival queen with her attendants and 'flower girls'. The 'flower girls' had dressed up to enter a *Daily Mail* competition held to celebrate the occasion.

141b. The winners of the Coronation Festivities Procession First Prize. They are dressed to show the countries of the British Empire.

141c. The mayor and mayoress, Mr. and Mrs. Robert Druitt, officially opening the coronation celebrations in 1911.

142a. Christchurch Regatta, held on 11 August 1909. This was revived on the initiative of the mayor of Christchurch, Cllr. D. Galbraith. As well as a boat race, there were swimming events, tug-of-war in punts and a fair. In the evening there was music, decorated boats, decorations and illuminations, and a dance was held at the *King's Arms Hotel*.

142b. The Canadian Canoe Men's Doubles (without co race being held during t regatta of 20 August 1913.

142c. Another element of the regatta was the fair. The showman's tractor in the foreground is thought to be a Brown and May, made in Devizes.

3a, b & c. Peace celebrations held on Saturday 19 July 1919. The streets of Christchurch were decorated with banners and flags to celebrate the end of the First World War and the return of local men from fighting at the front. The enormous procession through the main thoroughfare of the town and the size of the crowds that turned out to watch give an indication of the happy mood of the event. As well as the usual galas and competitions, a large bonfire was lit in the evening on Warren Head.

CHRISTCHURCH PEACE CELEBRATIONS, JULY 19, 1919.   [Geo. Moss, Photo., Christchurch

144.   A circus visiting the town in August 1921. It was owned by R. Fossetto and took place in a field behind Rotten Row. Circuses were a popular event in Christchurch and were often held in the meadows near the town.

145.   A reminder of Christchurch's smuggling past. This play was entitled *Contraband* and the actors are dressed to represent dragoons and excise men.

146.   Admiral Sir Edmund Lyons (1790-1858), Baron of Christchurch. Edmund Lyons was born at Burton in 1790 into a naval family. After a distinguished career, during which he became Commander in Chief of the Black Sea Fleet, he was received at Christchurch to a hero's welcome. Triumphal arches from Purewell to Bargates were erected and houses and shops decorated to mark the occasion in 1856.

147. George Ferrey, Burgess of Christchurch during the late 19th century. Together with his brother, William, he owned a tailor's, woollen draper's and hatter's in the High Street. The Ferrey family were in business in Christchurch from 1760 until 1936.

148. The Rev. T.H. Bush, vicar of Christchurch from 1884-1909. He lived at the Red House for a number of years and it was he who coined the name 'Red House' after the colour of the bricks used in the building. It was also Rev. Bush who knocked down several of the walls of the former workhouse, reducing it to its present size and creating the gardens.

149. Linwood Pike, beadle of Christchurch, *c.*1880. Mr. Pike was clerk to the Rural District Council for the highways, vestry clerk and income tax collector amongst other roles.

150. 'Poor Douglas Rushton of Lane's in Church Stree
Douglas Rushton lived with the Lane family, who were groce
How poor he was and why he is in the clerk's uniform own
by Linwood Pike is not known.

151. Samuel Bemister, mayor of Christchurch three times
between 1890 and 1900 and also on four other occasions. His
family were coal merchants who had premises next to the
Town Hall in the High Street.

2. Herbert Edmund Miller, verger of the priory church. The
Miller family lived at the Red House for a few years. A number
of the photographs in this book are the work of H.E. Miller.

3. Herbert Druitt (1876-1943) was a local antiquarian who
collected vast quantities of material throughout his life. His
over-riding aim was to create a museum, library and an art
gallery in the town. Although he managed to open a couple of
rooms in the Red House for a few years, he did not achieve his
lifelong ambition. After his death it was discovered that the
buildings left by him were filled from floor to ceiling with
mainly unsorted and unprovenanced material and a lot of his
collections were disposed of. The remainder form the core of
the collections of the Red House Museum today. He is on the
left of this photograph (dated 11 March 1940) with Mr. Maurice
Wilkinson.

154. A view from the priory, looking down Church Street, to the junction with the High Street and Castle Street. In the background the chimney of Christchurch Electricity Company can be discerned and the steeple of the United Reformed church in Millhams Street. Tram lines can just be made out in Church Street, dating the photograph after 1905.

155.   The village of Iford, 1904. Until a bridge was built at Tuckton in the 1880s, the bridge seen to the right of the photograph was the only means of crossing the Stour by road. A new bridge was built in 1932 to ease growing traffic problems.

156.   Looking east along Purewell. *c.*1920. The expansion of Christchurch during the 19th century absorbed Purewell into the town. The shops on the left of the photograph were run by George Cox, bootmaker; Herbert James Dibley, newsagent; and George Andrew Sands, draper. One of the headlines outside the newsagent's reads: 'British at Danzig' (*Daily News*) Danzig, now Gdansk, a port in Poland, became a free city under the League of Nations in 1919. It was later annexed by Germany in 1939, an event that precipitated the Second World War.

57. Somerford Grange, the home of John Draper, the last prior of Christchurch Priory. After the dissolution of the monasteries, John Draper lived here until his death in 1552. The Grange was the Manor House of Somerford and its land stretched as far as the borders of the New Forest. Somerford Grange was pulled down in 1938 to make way for housing estates.

58. A view of Stanpit, looking towards Mudeford, *c*.1930. The public house on the right is the *Ship in Distress* which became notorious, along with the *Eight Bells* in Christchurch, as both public houses were well known smugglers' haunts.

286 STANPIT, CHRISTCHURCH

159.   Mudeford Quay seen from Mudeford Spit at the turn of the 20th century. The narrow channel of water between them is known as the Run. Mudeford, literally 'Muddy ford', is still an important area for fishing. The buildings in the centre date from the 17th century and were used by coastguards a century later at the height of smuggling activities in Christchurch. They are known as the Dutch Houses or Haven House. The more modern building to the right is the *Haven Inn*, which is a public house today.

160.   The *Nelson Hotel*, Mudeford, *c.*1930. The landlord at this time was Gilbert Allen. Mudeford was the home of Sir George Rose, a former Lord of the Manor of the Borough. A visit by George III helped to make the village a popular destination for the gentry from London.

161. Wick Ferry, which took foot passengers across the Stour from Christchurch to the village of Wick. Until the Tuckton bridge was built in the 1880s this was the only means of crossing to the Bournemouth side. Pontins holiday camp has since been built on the site of the Christchurch landing.

162.	Burton Triangle, at the end of Martin's Hill Lane, c.1910. Burton village is now separated from Christchurch by a busy by-pass and has grown considerably.

63.   A view of Staple Cross, showing the business premises of Mr. Kerly, saddler. The building on the right was formerly
public house, known as *The Pineapple*. For a while the Kerly family ran both the public house and the saddlery business.
he railway bridge in the background still stands; the road running under it leads to Ringwood. Staple Cross is also
eparated from Christchurch by the by-pass.

164.   Highcliffe Castle. This Gothic-style home of the Victorian Romantic era was built in the 1830s for Lord Stuart of
Rothesay. The original architect was William Donthorne who also rebuilt the West Gate at King's Lynn. After his
dismissal, the work was completed by Augustus W.N. Pugin. Most of its grandeur was destroyed during a fire in 1967.

65. Throop Mill, which finally stopped grinding corn in 1974. The mill dates back at least to the 16th century and alternated between grinding corn and grist (probably malt).

66. Heron or Hurn Court, near Blackwater and East Parley, the ancestral seat of the Earl of Malmesbury, the Lord of the Manor of Christchurch.

167.   Blackwater Ferry towards the end of the 19th century. This was near the Bournemouth spur road crossing of the Stour. The site is almost unrecognisable today.

68. A view of Christchurch Harbour from the quay. The harbour is sheltered from almost all angles by sand banks or pits which have built up in the area through longshore drift. Part of a poled punt can be seen right of the picture; these were used to cross the shallow waters of the harbour.

69. Hengistbury Head, an evocative name given to the headland in Victorian times. The name is derived from a legend which tells of the landing of Hengist and his brother Horsa on the head in A.D. 449 and the subsequent uprising of the king of Kent. From this site, worked flints from the Old Stone Age (Palaeolithic) have been found in some quantity. Other archaeological evidence points to the occupation of the head during Roman times. More recently, in the 19th century, ironstone was mined here by the Holloway family. Although Hengistbury Head is now part of Bournemouth, it protects the harbour of Christchurch and is still a popular destination for Christchurch residents and its visitors.

Bibliography

Barker, J., *Christchurch Barracks* (Bournemouth Local Studies, 1984)

Davey, S., *Christchurch in Old Picture Postcards* (European Library—Zaltbommel/ Netherlands, 1984)

Dear, G.D., *Christchurch—from Watermills to Waterworks Part III. Fulling Mills and Corn Mills,* Leaflet 319 (1975)

Druitt, H., *Christchurch Miscellany*

Hodges, M.A., *Prepared for Battle* (Michael Hodges, 1978)

Jarvis, K. and J., *Explore Christchurch* (1990)

Lane, M.P., *Christchurch: A Short Historical Guide to Christchurch* (M.P Lane, undated)

Lavender, R., *1000 Years of Christchurch* (Bournemouth Local Studies, 1977)

Marshall, G., *The Christchurch Handbook* (1897)

Page, W., *The Victoria County History of Hampshire and the Isle of Wight* (1912)

Popplewell, L., *Wick* (Bournemouth Local Studies, 1989)

Samuel, O., *On the Bridge* (Olive Samuel, 1991)

Tucker, W., *Reminiscences of Christchurch and Neighbourhood* (Bournemouth Local Studies, 1979)

White, A., *Christchurch through the Years: Bargates, Fairmile and Barrack Road* (Allen White, 1986)

White, A., *The Chain Makers* (Allen White, 1967)

White, A., *Christchurch Airfield, 40 years of Flying* (Allen White, 1987)

White, A., *Clingan House* (Allen White, 1971)

White, A., *Christchurch through the Years: Church Street and Castle Street* (Allen White, 1985)

White, A., *Square House c.1776-1958* (Allen White, undated)

White, A., *High Street Handbook* (Allen White, 1970)

White, A., *Christchurch Photographers, 1855-1915* (Allen White, 1966)

White, A., *Christchurch High Street through the Years* (Allen White, 1982)

Wood, M., *Christchurch Castle* (HMSO, 1956)

Young, J.A., *Southbourne and Tuckton Yesterday* (Bournemouth Local Studies, 1990)

Young, J.A., *Ringwood, Christchurch and Bournemouth Railway* (Bournemouth Local Studies, 1992)

Directories:

Tuckers' Christchurch Almanack, 1893 and later

Kelly's, 1880 and later

Post Office, 1832

Church Street, *c*.1840. Etching by Benjamin Ferrey, architect, 1810-1880.